A First Guide to
Painting and Drawing

A FIRST GUIDE TO PAINTING AND DRAWING

Consultant Editor:

JUDY MARTIN

Oxford University Press

H 099040 21

A QUARTO BOOK

Published by
Oxford University Press, Walton Street, Oxford OX2 6DP

Oxford New York Toronto
Delhi Bombay Calcutta Madras Karachi
Kuala Lumpur Singapore Hong Kong Tokyo
Nairobi Dar es Salaam Cape Town
Melbourne Auckland Madrid

and associated companies in Berlin Ibadan

Oxford is a trade mark of Oxford University Press

A CIP catalogue record for this book is available from the British Library.

ISBN 0 19 910045 4

This book was designed and produced by
Quarto Children's Books Ltd
The Old Brewery 6 Blundell Street London N7 9BH

Creative Director Nick Buzzard
Managing Editor Christine Hatt
Editor Patricia Seligman
Designer Hugh Schermuly
Design Assistant Trish Going
Photographers Paul Forrester, Ian Howes
Illustrators Judy Martin, Elisabeth Smith, Sharon Smith

The Publishers would like to thank the following for their help in the
preparation of this book: Tessa Paul, Karen Ball, Rebecca Herringshaw

Picture Acknowledgements
Quarto Children's Books Ltd would like to thank the following for supplying
photographs and for permission to reproduce copyright material:
Wayne Lankinen/Aquila: 84 centre

Typeset by Central Southern Typesetters, Eastbourne, Sussex
Manufactured in Hong Kong by Regent Publishing Services Ltd
Printed by Leefung-Asco Printers Ltd, Hong Kong

Contents

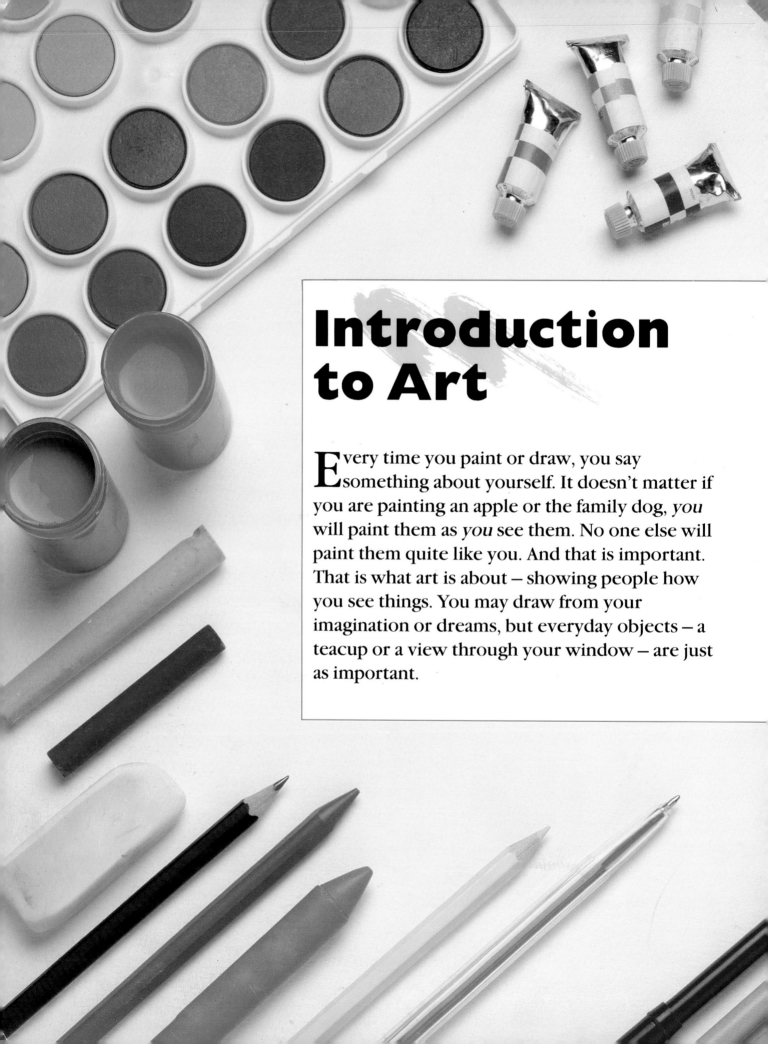

Introduction to Art

Every time you paint or draw, you say something about yourself. It doesn't matter if you are painting an apple or the family dog, *you* will paint them as *you* see them. No one else will paint them quite like you. And that is important. That is what art is about – showing people how you see things. You may draw from your imagination or dreams, but everyday objects – a teacup or a view through your window – are just as important.

In this book we show you different ways to paint and draw – with watercolour, poster paints, coloured pens, and pencils. All the artist's tools used are not expensive and can be found in good stationers. We look at exciting, fun ways to use these tools – dabbing paint on with a sponge or blowing it with a straw.

Along the way we also help you turn yourself into a 'real' artist, with tips on everything from mixing colours to using perspective. You may have thought of such skills as too hard, but we will show you how easy they can be. We suggest projects that give you the opportunity to practise your new skills, too. You will find that, with the help of this book, you soon start to paint pictures that you will be proud of.

Get Set

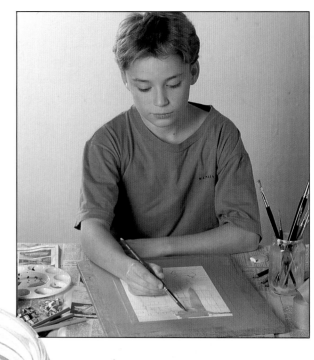

You have the ability to be an artist. In your paintings and drawings you can do what you want and express yourself freely. Sometimes your painting doesn't work. Sometimes it turns out better than you expected. By trying out all the different pencils, pens, and paints, you will find out what they can do. But first of all you need somewhere to paint.

▶ Clean Water
You will have discovered that if the water you dip your brush into is dirty, your painting will be dirty. So, clean your brush well between colours and change your water as often as possible. When you have rinsed and dried your brushes, store them upside down in a dry jar.

▲ Space to Create
You can be an artist at your desk, at a table, or on your lap. Find something hard to put your paper on. If you do not have a table, use a board. Have all your equipment – pens, pencils, paints, water jars – next to you, where you can reach them easily without stretching across your paper. Artists work better in a good light – from a window or a lamp.

▲ Mixing Colours
This white plastic palette makes mixing colours easy, but an ordinary plate will do as well.

Paper Stretching

Have you noticed that watery paint sometimes makes the paper buckle and curl? You can stop this happening to good quality paper by stretching it with water before you paint on it.

1 Lay the paper on a board and measure out four strips of brown gummed paper tape, one for each side.

2 With a clean, damp sponge, wet the surface of the paper and carefully flatten it on the board. Stick it down with the gummed strips along each edge. Leave to dry. Now you have a piece of buckle-free paper.

Cheap, white paper is best for practising drawing, but it will buckle when you paint.

Which Paper?

In an art or stationery shop you will find lots of different kinds of paper – thick, thin, smooth, rough, tinted, white. They all feel different to draw and paint on. Thin, cheap paper is fine for practising drawing, but you will find white cartridge paper better for painting.

Look at the different papers here and see how they change the appearance of the orange paint stroke and the blue pastel mark we have tried out on each sheet. The cheap paper drinks up the paint so that the paint stroke loses its colour. Compare it with the darker colour and interesting 'edge' of the paintmark on the special watercolour paper. The pastel mark is broken up by the rough pastel paper.

Special watercolour paper for wet techniques is expensive but is worth it for good results.

Tinted pastel paper is rougher on one side than the other.

Standard cartridge paper from a sketch pad comes in different weights. You may need to stretch it (see this page) for watercolour.

Rough cartridge paper will give your paint and pencil marks a textured effect.

Choosing Paints and Brushes

Paints that you mix with water – watercolours, poster paints, and acrylics – are the easiest to use. They need not cost much to start with, although as you improve you may want to try more expensive paints that will have better, stronger colours. Oil paints are harder for the beginning artist to use well. They have not been included in this book.

Going Halves (1)

In this windsurfing scene, you can see the effects of delicate water-colour (top half). Poster paints (used in bottom half), useful, as their name suggests, for posters, are bolder and thicker.

Poster and Gouache

These paints are thicker and more pasty than watercolours. You will find that the more water you add, the lighter a colour gets. They dry lighter still.

Pans of Colour

Watercolours come in dry blocks or 'pans'. Unlike poster paints, they are delicate colours, and are best used with lots of water. You will find they dry lighter than they look at first, but you can always darken them by painting over another layer, once the first one is dry.

French ultramarine

Viridian

Cadmium red

Alizarin crimson

Tubes of Colour

Watercolour, gouache, and acrylic paints can be bought in tubes. Begin with a selection of ten 'starter colours' like these. Then add to your collection as you become more experienced.

Which Brush?

Brushes come in different sizes and shapes. The most common are 'flat', which are square, or 'round', which are shaped like a tear drop. They are made of anything from nylon 'hair' to hog bristle. You can tell the size of a brush by its number. No. 14 is the biggest, and No. 0 the smallest.

A large, flat brush useful for flat washes (see below).

A large round brush for broad areas of colour.

Use a small brush for touches of colour or highlights.

A round No. 5 brush is the best one to start with.

Laying a Wash of Colour

When you begin a painting, it is usually best to start with the background colour – the sky, or maybe a beach. Then, when this pale, watery wash is dry, you can paint your flowers, trees or hills over the top. You can lay a wash with watercolour, acrylics or poster paints.

1 Mix a lot of water and very little paint in a small dish. Load your brush and, starting at the top, move the brush evenly across the paper, from side to side.

2 You will find that a ridge of colour collects along the base of each stroke. Brush it away with the next stroke, moving the colour smoothly to the edge. Aim for an even wash of colour.

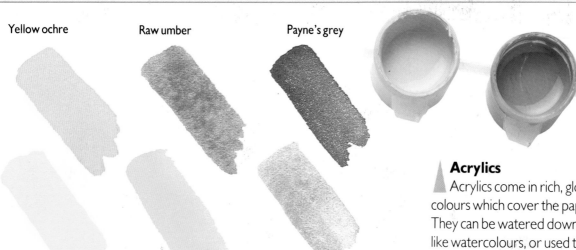

Yellow ochre

Raw umber

Payne's grey

Lemon yellow

Cadmium yellow

Cerulean blue

Acrylics

Acrylics come in rich, glossy colours which cover the paper easily. They can be watered down and used like watercolours, or used thickly straight from the pot or tube. Wash dirty brushes in water.

Soft 4B pencil

Standard HB pencil

Blackboard chalk

Chalk pastel

Oil pastel

Coloured pencil

Hard wax crayon

Water-soluble coloured pencil

Water-soluble crayon

Pencils, Crayons, and Pastels

Try painting and drawing with any colours you can lay your hands on. Pencils, crayons, and pastels all have their different uses. Coloured pencils are hard and dry, and travel well in pencil cases. You will find some new ways to use them on this page. Wax crayons are not just for toddlers. For a start, they combine well with paints for some fun effects (see pages 32–33). Pastels can be chalky or oily. Blend them with your fingers or use them like pencils.

Top Marks

The look of your picture will depend on the type of pencil or crayon you use. By trying them out, you can see what suits you best. Here we show you how different the marks can be.

Just Add Water

Some pencils and crayons can be used dry or wet. Water blends or spreads the colour, as in paint. You can either apply a wet brush to marks you have made on the paper, or dip the crayon in water and then draw with it. Experiment by copying the colour triangle on pages 24–25 using both pencils and crayons. You will soon see how different they are.

Mixing Exercises

As with paints, you can mix dry colours to create different colours or hues. But if you cannot mix them with water like paints, you have to use other ways like overlapping layers, or mixing dots of colour, as shown opposite. With pastels you can mix by gently blending colours together with your finger. Use these ideas for shading.

▲ Colour Mixing

You can mix dry colour by dotting colours side by side. Seen from a distance, your eyes will then do the mixing for you. Dots of red and yellow will appear as orange, or blue and yellow as green.

▲ Shading

With pencils, you can make dark or light shading just by pressing harder or softer. Practise this shading technique with free, sweeping strokes. Start by pressing hard, then let the stroke get softer.

▲ Cross-Hatching

These criss-cross lines are useful for shading. When you are cross-hatching like this, try using two colours so that you are mixing the colour at the same time.

▲ Going Halves (2)

See how chalk and oil pastels can make your picture look quite different. Oil pastels (above) make a strong mark. Chalk pastels (below) are drier and softer. Try both to see which you like better.

1 Try mixing pencil, crayon, or pastel by overlapping one colour with another. Here we begin with a purple pencil, starting dark and getting lighter.

2 Now add the second colour, overlapping the first one to start with. Start light and get darker. Where the two colours combine, a third colour appears.

▲ To mix pastels, shade two blocks of colour side by side. Now rub your finger gently across the blocks to form a third.

17

A fine tip for line drawing.

A broad felt-tip to fill in areas of colour.

A water-soluble pen with brush tip.

The type of useful, multi-purpose pen you find in a set.

A trusty ball-point for all types of drawing.

Picking Pens

Felt-tip and fibre-tip pens are cheap to buy, bright in colour and easy to use. If you are designing something to catch the eye – a poster or a birthday card – then these pens are the answer. You can buy inexpensive sets with standard-sized tips in a good range of colours. It is also useful to have some thin-tipped pens for linework, and some thicker ones for filling in areas of colour.

Mixing Pens

You will find that you can make some interesting effects by mixing colours with your felt-tip and fibre-tip pens. Once the marks have been made, waterbased inks can be mixed on the page with a wet brush. However, they will take a while to dry. Spirit-based inks dry almost immediately and do not run together so easily, so are better for cross-hatching.

Yellow over blue

Red over blue

Yellow and blue over red

Overlapping Colours
The ink in many types of felt-tip is transparent. This means you can lay one colour over another to create further colours. Experiment with your colours and see what unexpected hues you can produce.

Crossed Lines
By cross-hatching lines of different colours, you will create the illusion of a new colour. Look how this technique has been used in the drawing of fruit above.

Felt-Tip Fun

Look how clever you can be with felt-tip pens. Water has been painted on to make shadows and for the sea. Old, nearly dry, pens are useful for textured effects, as on the towel.

Pen Friends

Ball-point pens are fun to sketch with and they are easy to carry around. They produce a good smooth line that you can make darker or lighter by pressing harder or softer. Take care to start at the top of the page and work down or you may smudge the ink.

Spots Before the Eyes

By dotting and spotting colours together, you can create a whole range of colours and textures. This technique is called pointillism and can be done well with felt-tips.

Looking at Shape

We recognize things by their shape. But sometimes this shape can seem too complicated to draw. One way to tackle this problem is to 'fit' a difficult shape into a simple one, as shown below. Remember that an object changes its shape depending on where you look at it from. As a new artist, you must learn to see the shape in front of you as it really is, not as you expect it to be.

Changing Shape

You have to think hard when you are copying a shape because it changes as you move around it. Keep looking up to the object and back to your paper to check you have it right.

Circle
To draw any object that is basically a circular shape, such as an apple, draw a circle first. Then see how the outline of the object differs from the circle. This should make it easier to draw.

Square
You may think a cushion is square, but it will never be quite regular. Use the square to guide you, but notice how the outline of the cushion bursts out of the square or doesn't quite touch its edges.

Rectangle
A rectangle can be the basis for a car, a house, or a loaf of bread.

Triangle
By drawing a triangle first, you will find it easier to make a jug symmetrical.

Cup Watch

Seen from above, the rim of the cup is a circle – but it doesn't look much like a cup! Viewed from the side, the cup's rim becomes an ellipse, or squashed circle. Now you can recognize it!

Tricky Tyre

Look how the shape of the tyre changes from different angles. Side on, it is round, but from everywhere else, it is an ellipse. Try drawing from various viewpoints (far left) to practise this!

Easier Than It Looks

This test will show how you can train yourself to look at shapes and outlines. Study the small picture above but, with a pencil, copy the upside-down illustration (right). Turned upside down, the girl's face becomes simply a pattern of lines that is easier to copy.

Light and Shade

Toning Up

A pencil can make light or dark marks on paper. Artists say that these marks vary in tone, or tonal value. In these three strips, the tone varies from dark at the top to light at the bottom. With a pencil (left and centre), you reduce the tone by pressing less hard. In the paint strip (right) the tone is reduced by adding white.

We do not need to feel something to know its shape. An apple is round, a box is square. We understand their form without touching them because we can see shadows curve round the apple, while on the box the shadow falls straight down. Artists say that light and shade 'model' the shape. If you want your painting or drawing to look real on a flat page, you need to use shadows and highlights to show the shapes of the objects and make them three-dimensional.

Model Shadows

Light 'models', or gives shape to objects. Highlights are created where the light falls, while surfaces hidden from the light are cast into shadow.

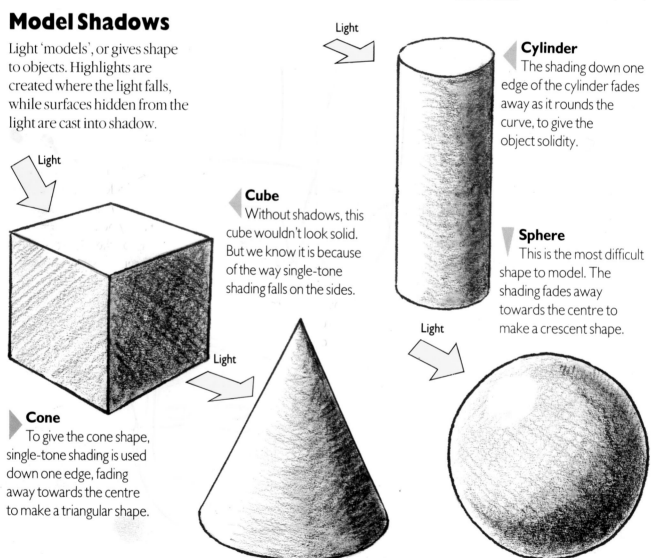

Light

Cylinder
The shading down one edge of the cylinder fades away as it rounds the curve, to give the object solidity.

Light

Cube
Without shadows, this cube wouldn't look solid. But we know it is because of the way single-tone shading falls on the sides.

Sphere
This is the most difficult shape to model. The shading fades away towards the centre to make a crescent shape.

Light

Cone
To give the cone shape, single-tone shading is used down one edge, fading away towards the centre to make a triangular shape.

Light

22

Seeing the Light

Always look carefully to see where the light is coming from – the light source. Remember to add the highlights on the side where the light first touches the object and shade the side furthest from the light source (see right). Cast shadows are affected by the direction and angle of the light source as shown below: (1) high light source from left (2) low light source from behind.

▲ **Wrong**
Look again. The light strikes the pepper grinder from the right. So that is where the highlights should be.

▲ **Right**
Now it's right. Here the highlights are brightest where the object is closest to the light source.

Shaping with Colour

You have seen that light and shade can be used to make objects appear solid. Colour can be used to do this too, as this drawing of an apple shows.

3 With a darker colour, shade the apple, fading gently into the centre. Finally, add the shadow cast by the apple on the ground.

2 Fill in the basic colours, leaving white areas for the highlights, to suggest shine.

1 With a circle as your basic shape, use a pencil to draw the outline of an apple.

23

Looking at Colour

Clever use of colour can add interest to any painting. As a new artist, you need to understand how to mix three colours – red, blue, and yellow – to make almost any other colour you can think of. Because all the others are made from them, these three are called primary, or first, colours. You also need to learn how really to see the colour in a scene – the sea is not always blue or the grass green – so that you can paint it well.

Getting Lighter
Different media are 'lightened' in different ways. Watercolour (far left) becomes lighter as you add more water. Gouache (centre) can be made paler with water or white paint. With a pencil (left), the tone gets lighter the less you press.

Colour Surprises
You need not add black to darken a colour. In fact, black often just makes a colour dull. Yellow can be darkened by adding just a touch of purple, green by adding a dash of red, orange by adding a dash of blue.

Yellow

Orange

Red

Green

Purple

Blue

Three Colours
Try to copy this triangle. It will help you to understand how to mix colours. On a palette, start with a blob of yellow. Then add red, a little at a time. (You should always add a darker colour to a lighter one.) The colour will change through orange to red. Now start again with a second blob of yellow and add blue. Finally, start with a blob of red and add blue.

24

Black-and-White Vision

If we look at a black-and-white photograph of a painting, we can judge the tonal values of the colours used – just how 'black' or 'white' they are. Bright summer sun, as in this scene, makes dark shadows and bright highlights. Try painting an object – a jug say – with mixes of only black and white.

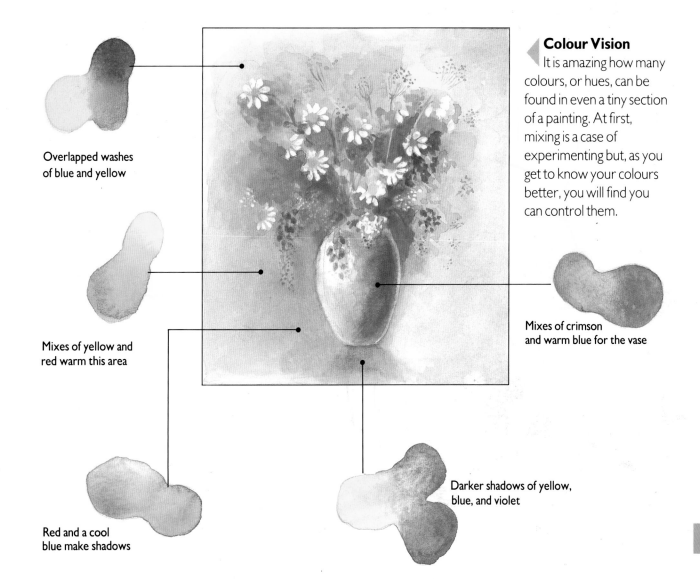

Overlapped washes of blue and yellow

Mixes of yellow and red warm this area

Red and a cool blue make shadows

Colour Vision
It is amazing how many colours, or hues, can be found in even a tiny section of a painting. At first, mixing is a case of experimenting but, as you get to know your colours better, you will find you can control them.

Mixes of crimson and warm blue for the vase

Darker shadows of yellow, blue, and violet

Composing your Picture

You are searching for a view to sketch. Everything seems big, crowded, and messy. So, look for a small corner of the scene. Find one that has less in it but some unusual shapes, different lines, colours, and textures. What you are doing is arranging your view. You can choose what you want to include and the angle you view it from – high up or low down. The final arrangement is called your composition.

▶ Simple Sketches
In your sketchbook, try out lots of different views of the same scene. They need only be small, like the ones shown here.

Again, the vertical masts and houses look better in this 'portrait' frame.

This little boat with its tall mast begs to be framed in the 'portrait' shape.

A 'landscape' frame suits this panoramic view out to sea.

▲ Messy View
A jumble of boats, this harbour view is a mess. Where should you start? The solution is to walk around your subject a bit. Find a detail, here maybe a single boat, and view it from different angles until you find a happy balance of form and space.

Viewed from an angle, this row of boats invites you deep into the picture.

The main lines here are horizontal, from side to side. So a 'landscape' frame is the obvious choice.

▲ Shaping Up
When you sketch a scene, you can choose to make it a 'landscape' shape, which is wider than it is tall, (above and left), or 'portrait' which is taller than it is wide, like those at the top. You will find it makes a difference to the balance of the composition.

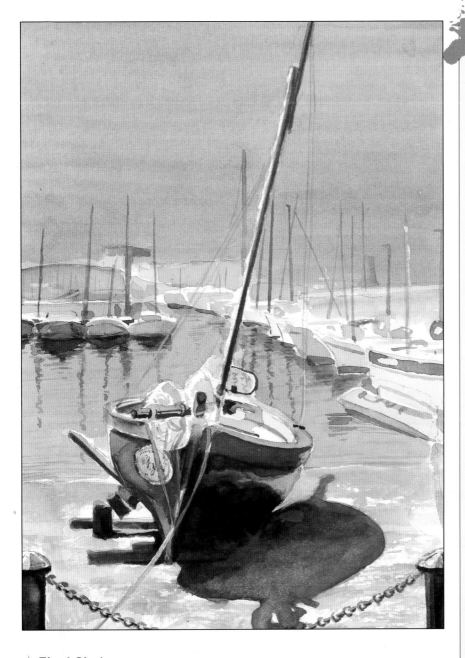

Framing the View

A viewfinder is an excellent device used by artists. It is a type of portable frame you can carry with your sketchbook. If you look through it, you frame the scene and see how it would look on your page. You can also try out landscape and portrait shapes and see which looks better.

Final Choice
This was the artist's final choice for the composition. Would you have chosen it? Can you see how the artist walked round the harbour view in the muddled photograph on the opposite page and focused on this boat, framing it with the water behind?

To make your own viewfinder, take a piece of paper or card 15 × 18 cm (6 × 7 in), and cut out a rectangle 10 × 13 cm (4 × 5 in) from the centre. Two L-shaped cards can be even more useful. They can be held as shown above, and the size of the frame adjusted to suit you. Try it out around the room where you are making it. Doesn't the world look different?

27

Keeping a Sketchbook

A sketchbook is fun to keep. If you carry one around with you and use it all the time, you will find it becomes more like a diary. It is where notes, ideas, and information are stored – faces, places, a funny dog, an interesting door. When you sit down to paint, you can remind yourself of the things you have seen, or kick-start your imagination.

◄ Which Sketchbook?
You may like to have a ringbound sketchbook as they are easier to fold back. Or one with a hard cover – useful when you cannot find a surface to support your work on. It doesn't need to be huge – a pocket-sized one is fine.

▼ Just Testing
Test out techniques and different paints, pencils, and crayons in your sketchbook. Then when you want to produce a particular effect, you can look back at these pages.

Ringbound,
pastel-paper
pad

Small,
rough-surfaced pad

Hardback,
bound sketchbook

28

Squaring Up

When you want to use a small sketch as the basis for a large drawing or painting, you may find it difficult to copy your sketch in a larger size. By squaring it up, as shown here, you copy one square at a time so that you keep your picture in proportion.

With a ruler, carefully measure and draw up a grid of regularly-spaced squares over your sketch. Now, on your drawing paper, draw up a similar grid with the same number of squares, but make it as big as you need – twice or three times the original size. Next, copy your sketch, square by square.

When, say, you are copying the line of the trunk, mark where it crosses the edge of a square. Try and pencil it in with the same flow as the original.

Try It Out
Draw freely. Try and grasp the shape and outline to start with. Don't tear up your 'mistakes', they can give you ideas later on. Try taking a sketch across two pages.

Odds and Ends
Your sketchbook can also be a scrapbook, full of ideas and images. Paste postcards, magazine pictures, photographs, among your own drawings to build a busy artist's reference book.

29

At Home

Once you discover the different characters of your pencils, pens, and paints, you will need something to copy – a subject. You do not need to go further than your own home. Look around you. Your bedroom should be a good place to start. How about drawing the crumpled shirt on the floor of your room, or maybe the neatly folded one on your chair? Furniture and covers can make good subjects and backgrounds as you will see. Chairs and tables can be arranged simply, but look for an original viewpoint. Or you could paint a portrait of your favourite soft toy on the bed.

What about the kitchen? There are so many odd-looking gadgets to study here, not to mention fresh food in the fridge and packets and tins in the cupboards. Everyone draws apples, so make yours more interesting by taking a bite out of it or cutting it in half.

Then, of course, you may be able to persuade your family pets, or even your family, to pose. If not, try and catch them when they are asleep! We will be looking closely at people and the way they move, and give you tips about painting portraits. And to help you with your pets, we look at ways of painting fur, feathers, and scales.

Keep your sketchbook to hand so that you can record everything around you. This will give you a ready store of ideas and images.

Blot for a Bloom

Certain fruit, like grapes and plums, have a white powder on their skins called a bloom. You can give grapes a bloom with a tissue.

1 First paint in the grape colour – here, purple and green, allowed to run into each other.

2 Now, wind a tissue round your index finger. Blot up spots of surface paint, leaving the stained paper to form a soft bloom.

Food for Art

Once you start looking for things to draw and paint, you will stop thinking of fruit and vegetables as food and start seeing them in terms of form, colour, and texture – lumpy, bumpy cauliflowers, smooth, shiny tomatoes, curly lettuces. There are lots of artist's tricks to help you capture these wonderful forms and textures.

Apple Colours
The secret of this watercolour study is that the artist has built up the colour with layers of paint: first a wash of pale yellow, followed, when dry, by curving strokes of green and red, and then white gouache highlights.

Grape Variety
The artist has really looked at these grapes. No two grapes are exactly the same shape or colour. Note the bloom.

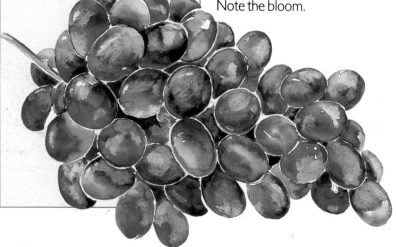

Wax Works

Wax repels, or resists, water, so if you paint watercolour over wax stripes, it only stays on the areas of paper without wax. This technique is called 'wax resist', and can be used to produce some interesting effects, as we show you here. You can use a candle for the wax, or wax crayons if you want the colour to show.

Waxy Orange
The highlight on the rough skin of this orange is the white of the paper, showing through the watercolour wash. The trick here is that textured, grainy paper was used, combined with the wax resist method described below.

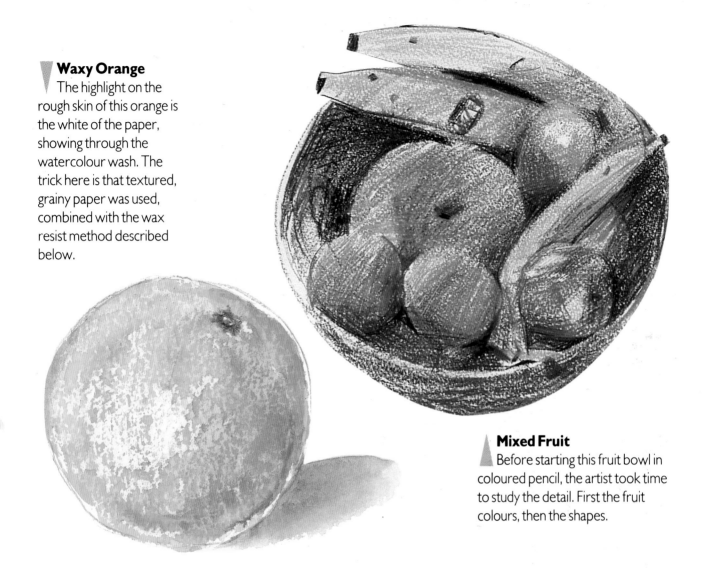

Mixed Fruit
Before starting this fruit bowl in coloured pencil, the artist took time to study the detail. First the fruit colours, then the shapes.

1 Draw the shape of a marrow very lightly with a pencil. Now, 'draw' in the pale stripes of the marrow skin with a white wax candle.

2 Mix a watery yellow with clean water. With a big, soft brush, wash the yellow over the whole marrow shape. Do you see how the wax resists the paint?

3 Let the yellow dry. Now make wax stripes over the yellow with the candle. Mix watery green and wash this over the marrow shape to finish your work.

Everyday Objects

Look around you and you will find lots of objects to paint and draw – pencils in a pot, an earthenware jug, or a bunch of keys. These household objects have interesting shapes and surfaces which can test your skills as an artist. A painting or drawing of such non-living objects is called a still life.

Watering-Can
Poster paints are good for hard, shiny surfaces. Paint dark shadows over a lighter base colour, then add white highlights.

Keys
The skill here is in the drawing of these complicated shapes. Watercolour has been added carefully, almost as an afterthought.

Bottle
Glass is always a challenge. Try using pastels which are easy to control when creating the reflections.

Working Sight Size

You will find it easier if you copy things the same size as you see them. This is called working sight size. It means you may have to go closer to what you want to draw to fill your page, or further away if it can't be fitted on the page. Move until you see the objects at the right size for your paper.

Candle
Oil pastels are well suited to the smooth texture of this candle. The surface is built up by working one colour into another.

Arranging Still Life

Objects from around the house make a good still life. Make several sketches before deciding on the final arrangement.

▼ This is one view of these household objects. The arrangement is rather unnatural.

▶ Now the pot is full of dark brown coffee, changing the balance of the composition.

▼ After sketching a number of views and arrangements, this composition was chosen for a detailed still life in poster paints.

▼ Try moving the objects around a bit. Coming closer in, the reflections on the pot become important.

Painting Glass

Glass reflects colours and distorts shapes seen through it. You will find it easier to paint a glass if you look at it as a jigsaw of coloured shapes.

1 Make an outline drawing in pencil, mapping out the coloured shapes in the glass. Wash in the background colours. Then start on the paler areas of colour.

2 Look at the shapes of the grey shadows and paint them in. Now add highlights in white, painting along a ruler for straight lines.

3 There are stronger shadows where the glass thickens at its base. Add little touches of dark grey here to increase the contrasts between light and shade.

35

Focus on Furniture

Furniture is practical. You use it every day. You sit on chairs, eat or work at a table, and sleep in a bed. So, it is easy to overlook the fact that furniture is also beautiful, intricate, even ugly. As you explore your home with sketchbook in hand, look at the furniture. You will be amazed by the interesting shapes and colours you will find.

▼ Sofa Shapes
Move the chair around and look for some unusual viewpoints. Here you can see the sofa through the back of the chair. Breaking up the sofa like this makes you look at it in a different way.

▲ New View
When you use a camera, you find yourself forced to see things in a new way. Soft, curved lines form the sofa arm. Harder lines are used for the wooden chair.

▶ Hard and Soft
Look at the shapes made by the curves and angles, but also capture the softness of the sofa in contrast to the hard chair.

Folding Fabrics

When sketching a room, you will probably find yourself drawing folding fabrics – curtains, a shawl over a chair or bed covers. Try not to see folds as straight lines on the material, look at each fold as a shape. Curtains will change depending on whether the light is shining on or through them. Try a tonal sketch (see pages 24–25) of a curtain to explore this.

1 Pencil in the outline of the curtain and the shapes of the folds. Paint in the background and shadow areas, leaving the highlights as white paper.

2 Once dry, apply the pattern across the folds, making sure that parts of it curve around the folds and 'disappear' behind them.

▼ Cutting In

Cutting the chair and sofa with the frame makes an almost abstract picture of shapes and spaces, rather than a sofa and chair.

▼ Camera Angles

You are so familiar with your own bedroom, it may be difficult to see anything interesting to draw. Use your camera and take photos from a variety of angles. Perhaps you might choose to focus on the angled view above.

▼ Artist's Choice

The artist chose this arrangement of cuddly toys against the screen. The different textures are captured with coloured pencils.

3 Now add the shadows. Then, with a fine brush, outline the deepest folds with black. Add white highlights to the outer folds where the light falls.

Project: Still Life

These peppers and aubergine, which you might find in your kitchen, make a good still life. Peppers are coloured so brightly, with shiny skins and unexpected forms. Aubergines are smoother, almost silky to touch. Surrounded by a softer fabric bag, these textures become the main challenge.

Think about your composition and take time to arrange the vegetables. Consider the source of light as this will affect the arrangement you choose. It may be from a lamp overhead, or natural light from a window. For this project, felt-tip pens were used, including the water-soluble type.

Quick Snap
A photograph of your chosen arrangement can be a useful reference.

Quick Sketches
Prepare by making some sketches to explore your arrangement. Try out different viewpoints, from above or with your nose level with the table.

1 When you have decided the still life is right, make a more detailed sketch and draw in the outlines with fine felt-tip pens.

Test Strip

It is sometimes difficult to tell how colours or mixes will look on your paper. So keep a corner of your sheet for testing them out.

2 Now add a foundation wash with water-soluble pens. First make a few marks on the paper. Then dip your finger in water and smooth out the colour.

3 Looking carefully at your still life, use the pens without water to build up strong areas of colour. Leave the highlights as the washed paper showing through.

4 Next, add the finer details of the stalks and shadows. Note how the background cloth has been built up with overlaid hatching in different colours.

5 The frayed tip of this damaged pen was useful here to draw the stalk of the aubergine.

▼ **Texture Contrasts**
What a success. The artist has captured the shiny textures of the vegetables and contrasted them with the soft fabric bag.

People Shapes

The trick with drawing people is to look at them as objects. Forget that you are sketching your sister or your grandmother. Just think of them as shape and form. People shapes are fascinating because they are always changing, always new. A sitting body takes on a new form when it stands, a squatting body is different from a sleeping body. Sketch your family as they move around the house.

▶ Slumped Figure
Sketch a person slumped in a comfortable chair. Observe the long sloping line of the back, and the sharp angles of the knees.

▲ Rectangular Pose
This person shape fits into a simple rectangle. Knees, elbows, and feet make precise angles.

Relative Sizes

It helps when you are drawing a person if you remember that the various parts of the body relate to each other, that the human body has standard proportions. As you can see in these drawings, in the adult man, the distance from neck to feet is six times the size of the head. But the proportions are different for the girl (head 1, rest of body 5) and the toddler (head 1, rest of body 3). You can use these standard proportions to help you with lengths of arms and legs, too.

Balancing Act
Study how the body changes in different positions. Here, with the weight on the right leg, the hips tilt one way and the shoulders the other.

In Shape
To help you draw figures, try fitting them into geometric shapes. In this tricky pose, notice the triangle made by the lap and the bent leg.

Triangular Shapes
Look at the spaces made between chair and body – the triangles at each shoulder, and in the small of her back and bottom. Sketch not a person, but lines and shapes.

A Quick Measure

You may like to draw your figure within grid lines, as shown in the box on the opposite page. But as a quick guide, to check that the body proportions are right, you can always use the top of your pencil.

Hold your arm out straight in front of you with the pencil upright in your hand. Align the top of the pencil with the top of the person's head and put your thumbnail on the pencil, level with the person's chin. Keeping your thumb in place, move the pencil down the body to see how many times the length of the head goes into the length of the body.

41

Moving Figures

Stick Shapes
Sketching people as stickmen will help you grasp the basic lines of a moving body.

Observe the line of the spine. Here it is a sharp curve.

Reaching up, the body is almost in a straight line. But notice the arch in the spine.

The parts of the body have a natural sense of balance. If the hips jut forwards, the shoulders go back.

The body changes shape very clearly when a person is crawling.

As an artist, you will develop a quick hand and a sharp eye so that you can capture movement. Do not worry about details of the body you are sketching, but look at the shape it makes as it bends, leaps, stretches, and crawls. You will begin to see how bodies shift their weight and hold their balance, the position of the shoulders in relation to the feet, or the angles of the hips and knees.

Basic Shapes
Train your eye to see the basic shape of a figure. This will help you catch the pose before the person moves. If you notice that these bending figures form triangles, your hand will quickly record the lines that the body makes within that shape.

Clothes in Action

The folds in people's clothing play an important part in creating a sense of movement in their bodies.

Moving Parts
The fluid pastel strokes used to show the play of light and shadow over these folds help to express the movement in this drawing.

Material Differences
Fabric imitates body movements. Some materials are thin and clingy, following every line of the body's form, such as in this T-shirt. Others, such as in this painter's overalls, are loose and bulky, creating heavy folds where the body bends and twists.

Body Lines
Notice how people place their arms and imagine the line of the spine. The tilt of the head and the slope of the shoulder are very important too.

Right Lines
You can see here how the artist has explored the line with his ball-point pen. He would have looked up at the figure and back at the paper again and again, drawing several soft lines for, say, the stomach before firming up the one that felt right.

43

Expressions

When you draw a face laughing or crying, certain lines change shape. We all know that the mouth turns up when we smile, but eyes change shape too.

▲ **Smile Lines**
A smile forces up the cheeks against the eyes making them crescent-shaped.

▲ **Angry Looks**
In anger, the mouth is small and straight and the brow furrows, drawing the eyebrows closer together.

▲ **Down in the Mouth**
An unhappy face has a wide, downward-sloping mouth and tilted eyebrows.

Making Faces

You can sketch a head and how it tilts and turns and then, with a few lines, fill in the eyes, nose, and mouth to make a 'face'. But to draw a face you know, your mother's, father's or best friend's, you need to observe carefully and record details. Are the eyes close together? What shape is the mouth? If you manage this, your 'face' then becomes a portrait.

½

½

▲ **Head Lines**
Like the body, the face has standard proportions. Notice how the forehead, nose, and chin fit into the head. You may well be surprised to find that the eyes come halfway down, and to see how close the mouth is to the chin line. Of course, as the head turns, these proportions stay the same.

▶ **Different Angles**
The proportions of the face change when seen at an angle from above or below. In the upturned face, the distance between the mouth and chin is exaggerated and the forehead appears shorter. The features of the downturned head run into each other and the forehead seems overlarge.

Flesh Tones

Skin is not simply 'black' or 'white', but many colours and tones in between. Everyone's skin is slightly different. Here, these flesh tints have been mixed in gouache from variations of the primary colours, plus white. But only a *touch* of each colour has been used.

PALE SKIN
Yellow   Blue–Green
Scarlet

MEDIUM SKIN
Yellow ochre   Ultramarine
Vermilion

DARK SKIN
Yellow   Violet
Red–Brown

Look Again
This is a good try, but can you see how the flesh is a bit flat and pink. The artist has not noticed how the skin has shadows and highlights – around the eyes, along the jaw line, around the mouth.

Well Done
Here the flesh tones are more subtle. The artist has used touches of violet and green for the shadows, and yellow and white for the highlights. Daring mixing captures the shape of the face.

Project: Myself

This project is about you. There is no better subject because you are always conveniently around, ready to pose. In this project, too, we will look more closely at how to use watercolour. It is a good medium for a portrait because it is a delicate, transparent paint which suits skin tones and textures. Now, what are you going to wear? Put on something which expresses your character – perhaps a favourite hat or T-shirt.

▲ Mirror Image
Position yourself close enough to the mirror to be able to see yourself clearly, but leave enough space on your work table to lay out your paints and brushes.

▲ Getting It Right
Before you start the portrait proper, try out different poses and outfits in the mirror and then do some colour sketches. You can then see what works best. The artist has chosen to do these sketches in coloured pencil and watercolour.

1 Once you have chosen the pose you like best, pencil in your outline and main details. Mark in the highlights to remind yourself to leave them unpainted. With a thick brush and watery paint, wash in the skin, hair, T-shirt, and background, painting round the highlights.

2 Once the first wash is dry, look for the shadows on your face, hair, and clothes. Now, add another layer of colour to these areas. Use the same colours as in step 1, but with less water. You may need to apply several layers, allowing each one to dry.

3 You are gradually building up the layers of paint over the shadow areas. The highlights are the white paper, the light parts the thin wash, the mid-shadows, more layers. Now work on the darker areas of shadow. With a fine brush, add details.

4 Add more detail with a finely pointed brush, as the artist is doing with the T-shirt stripes here. Relax your hand and don't worry if the line is not even — it won't be over the folds of clothes.

▶ **Spitting Image**
To finish, add touches of browny red to the lips, the corners of the eyes, the ear, and in the hair. It looks good.

Animal Art

Pets are good subjects to draw around the home because they are always there! Study them carefully when they are asleep and get to know their shapes. Animals often walk off or change position when you are drawing, so you will need to work fast. They are also quite tricky to draw accurately, but don't let this stop you trying. Remember, no drawing is wrong, but part of your way of learning to express your own talent.

◀ Pet Photograph
Your pet will not listen when you beg it to sit still while you sketch. Photographs will help you to study poses. Why not try drawing this mischievous cat.

▲ Sleeping Sketches
Whip out your sketchbook as your cat settles down to sleep. Move around your subject to sketch it from various angles. Use pencil or a water-soluble felt-tip washed with water.

Animal Shapes

To keep the parts of your pet in proportion, try looking at it as a series of geometric shapes. For instance, many dogs – terriers or spaniels – fit into a horizontal rectangle, with the head and legs, and even ears and tail, as smaller rectangles. Seeing your pet in this way will help you decide the relative sizes of the different parts of its body.

◀ This rabbit is a series of ovals of different sizes, from the body, to the head and thigh, right to the tiny tail.

▼ Capture the rough shape of your rabbit with ovals, then study it and see how the outline of your pet differs.

Stretch Sketch
Look at that stretch from the tip of the front paws to the base of the tail! You will see that the fur, like the clothes on a human, moves with the movement, emphasizing the action.

Head First
It might help you to capture this dog scratching for fleas if you imagine it in a triangle. Notice how the artist, using coloured pencils, shows the head with a lot more detail than the body. He has chosen this as the most important part of the drawing.

Three circles drawn one inside the other can be transformed into a mouse with the addition of a few details. Don't forget the whiskers.

49

Animal Hair and Fur

A Dry Brush

Some animals, like seals, have such short fur that drawing it is almost like drawing skin. Others are so furry that you can use all sorts of interesting techniques to portray the texture. Some media may seem easier to use for fur – pencils allow you to draw every hair. But you will find all media – paint, pastels, and crayons – have different advantages when you paint and draw animals.

With paint, you can copy the texture of fur very easily using the dry brush technique. Use thick paint, and not too much, so that the brush stays 'dry'. Different brushes will produce different types of 'fur'. Try them out.

▲ Dip your brush in the paint, then blot it fairly dry on tissue. Now, spread the bristles between thumb and finger as you drag the brush across the paper.

Rubbing Along
When using coloured pencil, you can use your eraser to create texture by rubbing out colour to make highlights. Try dragging the eraser along pencil lines to soften them for long, fine hair. Lots of short, lively strokes create this bushy tail.

Cat Coat
This cat's glossy, tortoiseshell coat was built up with layers of poster paint, using the dry brush technique (see left).

Furry Effects
Using different media – watercolour, felt-tip, and oil pastels – brings out different characteristics in these three mouse portraits.

With watercolour, the glossy coat of the mouse is painted with the dry brush method shown on the opposite page.

Fur Colours
With gouache and poster paint you can paint light over dark. Use a fine brush to paint the hairs in individual strokes over the basic colours.

The texture of the coat is shown with short strokes of colour using felt-tip pens.

In oil pastels, the fur highlights are scratched out with a needle.

Feathers and Scales

We are lucky to have such an extraordinary range of birds, reptiles, and fish to paint and draw. Feathers are beautiful, delicate forms which are good to sketch even on their own. But when you are drawing a bird, you don't have to paint in every one – nor every scale on a fish. The artist has to capture the texture and colour of large masses of feathers or scales with a few strokes, seeking out the details which make a particular bird or fish special.

Quick on the Draw
Birds tend to be restless so make numerous, quick sketches. Don't worry about getting it 'right' – just remember, the more sketches you make, the more confident you will become.

Bright Budgie
With gouache, the intricate feather patterns on this budgerigar are carefully marked out. It is the white highlights which give the feathers a texture you want to touch.

Goose Feathers
Fibre-tip pen is used to colour-sketch this goose. The impression of feathers is made through the simple black outline together with the flat grey shading in two tones.

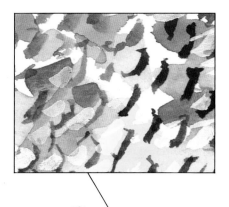

Scale Colours
Note the range of colour and tone in the watercolour patchwork with white paint highlights.

Lizard Outline
An artist can use the outline of an animal to give a clue to the texture of its skin. The slightly jagged edge of this lizard's back and tail hints at the unevenness of its scales.

Neck Detail
Over delicate washes of blue and green, the scales were added with a fine brush and brown paint.

Fish Finish
In the finished portrait, the goldfish looks shiny. Burnishing is great for scales.

Colour Polishing

You can 'polish' your colours – a technique called 'burnishing'. Use with coloured pencils or pastels.

1 Sketch the fish, then fill in with coloured pencils. Now rub over these colours with a white pencil to polish them and make them shimmer.

2 You can add more colour – use thick strokes. Polish this layer by rubbing it with a blunt knitting needle.

Scaly Snake
Dots of white paint form highlights over cross-hatched coloured pencil, giving a sheen to the scaly skin.

Project: My Pet

Making a portrait of your pet may sound easier than it is. As you have already found out, pets do not naturally stay still for very long. So get ready to do some quick sketches to capture the shape and position you want. Then you need to study your subject for colour and details only. For example, you can always study the eye when you get to that detail, even if your pet has moved from its original position. Chalk pastels were used for this rabbit portrait. Notice that blue has been used for the shadows rather than black or brown. This adds variety to the limited range of pastel colours. Pastels reproduce fur well and tinted pastel paper helps to make a pleasing portrait, too.

▼ **Photo Call**
Photographs of your rabbit can help with details, even if your rabbit is 'sitting' for his portrait.

1 Sketch the shape of the animal with light pastel strokes. Look carefully at the proportions of the head and body.

2 Use yellow, brown, and white pastels to draw the fur. Make quick, short strokes.

3 Be daring. The dark patches of fur can be drawn in with dark blue strokes.

4 To blend the pastels, use your finger to rub across the marks of colour. But be gentle and light in touch, otherwise the colours mix thick and muddy.

5 To soften the outline or lines of limbs, flick a brush very gently over the colour. Blow any loose powder away onto some newspaper.

▼ Resting Rabbit
A dark shadow round the bottom of the animal makes it 'sit' on the page. A few strokes of straw indicate his nest. Spray the finished pastel drawing with hair spray to stop it rubbing off.

Out on the Street

There are more exciting subjects for you to draw and paint out on the street. We live in buildings, shop in them, and work in them, so they make an obvious subject to paint. But not every town road or city street is a safe place to study the world from. You may have to draw and paint at a distance – from a window looking out on the street, or from a car. Quick sketches can be made from a bus or as you wait for a train.

But sometimes buildings seem too big to fit on the page. And, if you do fit them on, they look out of proportion. Luckily there are some 'tricks' to learn which will help you make your cityscapes look real. These 'tricks' include simple rules of perspective that will show you how to draw space and distance, and how to keep your drawing in scale. Once you have mastered simple perspective and can draw the structure of street life, then all you need to do is add those details which make our streets so lively – the people, dogs, cars, bicycles, and so on.

Armed with these tricks, you will find your village, town or city a much more interesting place to draw and paint.

One-Point Perspective

Perspective will help you draw buildings and streets so that the eye travels into the picture, rather than across it. Put in the horizon line (where the sky meets the flat land) at your eye level. This will be high or low depending on whether you are standing or sitting. Then make all horizontal parallel lines, say the sides of the street, run to a point on the horizon called the vanishing point.

▲ Centre of the Street
Lines meet at a point on the horizon. Above eye level, they move down, below, they move up.

▲ Side View
Move to one side of the street and the point on the horizon to which the lines vanish, the vanishing point, moves with you.

Drawing Buildings

Look carefully at any street scene. You will notice that distant buildings look smaller than buildings close to you, even if they are really about the same size. You need to remember this when you are drawing them. There are some simple rules to help you give a sense of distance to your pictures – the rules of perspective.

◀ Getting It Wrong
The artist here has not understood how perspective works, so the picture looks muddled and unreal. You cannot imagine walking down this street.

▲ Getting It Right
Here, you feel that you could amble down the road to the house at the end. All the horizontal parallel lines, that is those that are an equal distance apart (the top and bottom of the walls, for instance), meet at the vanishing point.

Two-Point Perspective

When you are drawing a building from one corner so that you can see two sides of it, you will need to use two-point perspective.

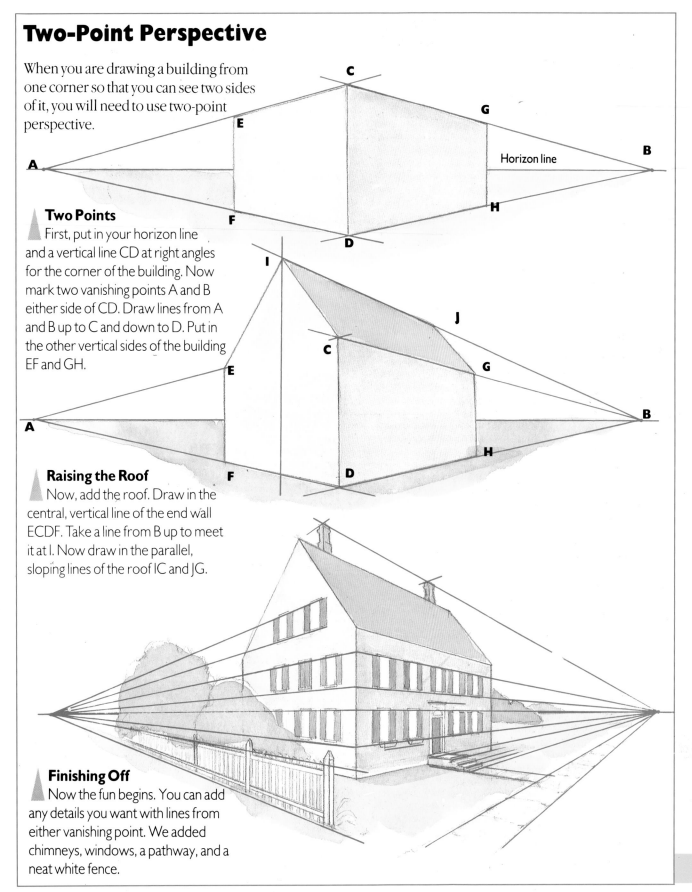

Two Points

First, put in your horizon line and a vertical line CD at right angles for the corner of the building. Now mark two vanishing points A and B either side of CD. Draw lines from A and B up to C and down to D. Put in the other vertical sides of the building EF and GH.

Raising the Roof

Now, add the roof. Draw in the central, vertical line of the end wall ECDF. Take a line from B up to meet it at I. Now draw in the parallel, sloping lines of the roof IC and JG.

Finishing Off

Now the fun begins. You can add any details you want with lines from either vanishing point. We added chimneys, windows, a pathway, and a neat white fence.

Brick-Work

You do not have to paint in every brick in a wall. You just need to give an impression. Try sponging on watercolour to create this effect.

1 Apply a wash of red-brown over sketched brickwork. Now darken the odd brick with further layers of colour.

2 Once dry, dip a sponge in brown paint and dab it over the brickwork. This creates the mottled texture of brick.

3 With a fine brush and brown paint, mark in the lines – not every one, and not ruler-straight.

House Portraits

When you paint a house, it is rather like doing a portrait of a person. You need to look at the small details that make it different from other houses – the brickwork, tiles on the roof, or window boxes. Your close observation of these details, and of the fall of light and shade on the building, will give your picture life and form.

Window Study
The more you study details, the more you learn which lines are important to the form and which lines you can leave out. For example, before you plan a painting of a building, study a window. Then, when you paint the whole house, you will know which few important lines you need to hint at the form of the window. This study reveals more than just shutters and frames. It depicts the fall of shadows, the colour reflections in glass panes, and the curtains. Go outside and focus in on a window in your home, or stay inside and paint a neighbour's window.

Painting a Portrait

Try painting a portrait of a house you know and like well – maybe your own. Work out the perspective (see pages 58–59) and then add the details.

Roof Shadows
The shadow cast by the gable gives form to this part of the roof.

Window Reflections
A row of windows, but each one different. The reflections add variety.

Economy of Detail
See how this picket fence is only hinted at with clever touches of green.

Light Steps
The fall of light is important even in details like the steps.

People Outdoors

People outdoors are usually on the move – shopping, rushing along, jogging or walking. You have seen how to capture movement on pages 42–43. Now you can learn to draw people moving around outdoors as part of a larger composition. As you will see, there are various artists' tricks to indicate action.

Giants or Pygmies?

The way we see is strange – that much we have learnt. Things change depending on where you see them from. Even the tallest person looks short if he is far away. Use perspective lines (see pages 58–59) to fit humans into the scale of buildings and streets.

Whizzing Along
'Whizz' lines, showing the direction of movement, give a strong impression of air rushing past the cyclist as he pedals forward with great speed.

Speeding Along
With this speedy skateboarder, the colour has been allowed to 'bleed' outside the outline, behind her. It has a similar effect to 'whizz' lines (above).

Cut For Action

There is a very clever tip that will help you give a strong feeling of movement to the people in your pictures. If a body is 'cut' by the frame, it looks as if that body is moving away, right out of the picture. Or perhaps it is moving into the picture, leaving a feeling of space beyond the frame.

People Practice
Before starting on a scene with figures in it, like the market below, you may like to sketch a few possible characters – such as this stall-holder and woman shopper.

Market Scene
Your sketchbook should be full of people moving through streets or markets with notes about scale and perspective. Now is the time to compose a more finished sketch, like this market scene in coloured fibre-tip pens.

Moving Crowd
Here bodies are half bodies. Some are reduced to just head and shoulders, as the frame cuts into them. So the crowd moves.

One Way
In this scene, there is only one line of movement, so that your eye is drawn horizontally across the picture.

Action Angles
Angled, receding lines of perspective, combined with a half figure cut by the frame, give a strong feeling of movement.

Project: Marathon

Now you are ready to tackle a crowd scene and put your new skills into practice. After all, you have sketched lots of figures and can create an impression of people moving with just a few well-chosen lines. This project is worked in gouache. The colours are strong and suit the bold approach of the artist. It is easy to correct mistakes with this medium, but let each colour dry before working over it. The street has a sharp perspective which, coupled with the frame cutting the figures in the foreground, makes it seem as if the runners are bursting forward out of the picture. The artist worked from both sketches and photographs.

▼ Running Figure
In a crowd scene, you won't need detailed studies of each figure. But, by making such drawings, you will learn to refine the line down to the few important ones needed.

1 Put a paper frame around your picture to keep the edges clean. Now, with a fine brush and black paint, outline the running figures. Make them all different, with more detail in the foreground.

2 Indicate buildings with a flat, grey paint. For leafy trees, paint green areas. Then take a sponge, dip it in yellow-green, and sponge over.

3 Fill in flesh tones on faces (see pages 44–45 for colour hints). In the foreground, paint arms and legs too. The black outline is important, so paint carefully.

4 Next, add the clothing. Not every detail, just a quick dab here for a red cap, and a touch of yellow there for a T-shirt. Use clear colours to enliven the scene.

5 Now lift the paper frame away. Your painting will have sharp, clean edges and is ready to exhibit.

Motion Picture
With a few black lines and clever patches of paint, you have created a scene that is busy and full of movement. You have had to work fast because gouache dries quickly, but the end result is worth your effort.

Landscapes

You don't have to live in the country to love the way trees are shaped and the colour of sunlight across hills, or enjoy the way nature changes with each season. A city park or even your own garden lets you enjoy the natural world, and, as an artist, you will want to put it all down on paper. Much of what you have learnt about perspective and scale is useful when drawing a landscape. Perspective lines can be ruled to plot the position of an avenue of trees.

But you will notice new things — that colours and textures change over distance and that perspectives seem different — because there is more sky and wider space in the country. The sky plays an important part in a landscape. It can often take up half your painting. The more you study the sky and clouds, the more you will find to inspire you. Clouds can be a subject in themselves — angry storm clouds or wispy summer clouds in a blue sky.

If you need photographs of the countryside to paint from, try magazine advertisements. They can give you ideas for dramatic combinations of weather, season, and landscape.

Open Spaces

In a landscape, the rules of perspective are still important. Trees get smaller as they disappear into the distance, so you can use perspective lines to work out their relative heights. But there are other ways of creating space in your landscape painting, such as through colour and tone. Even when you experiment with an imaginary landscape, you will be amazed to see how careful choice of colour changes your work.

Natural Scale

How do you fit people into the landscape? The answer is, in the same way as you fit them into a city scene – through perspective.

Rule in guiding perspective lines to show the horizon and vanishing point. You will find the right scale when you fit your figures and trees into the lines.

Horizons

The horizon in nature is not always obvious. It is the line where the sky meets the flat land or sea. But the horizon in your picture is still fixed by your eye level. Rules of perspective still apply – below your eye level, lines move up to the horizon. Above eye level, lines move down. And there are vanishing points.

Moving Horizons
The horizon changes when you move. Here the horizon is low down, so you are probably seated.

Far Horizon
You are high up. The horizon is far away and high on your page. The eye is taken to the horizon, not through receding lines, but through repeated horizontal bands of colour and contrasting tones.

Skyline
The horizon line here is the imaginary one where the sky meets the *flat* land, at the end of the plain.

Low Horizon
To make a dramatic picture, the eye level is low, and the cliffs soar above you.

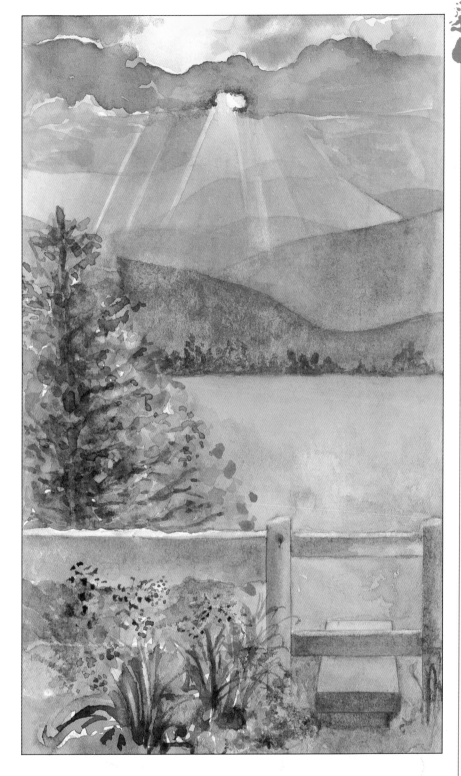

Making Space

You can use colour and tone to help you create a feeling of space in your landscape painting. Strong, warm colours with bright highlights and dark shadows bring objects forwards into the foreground. Softer tones and colours take them back.

In this picture, the house is painted in strong red-brown and comes forward from the pale blue background.

Using the same colours, but reversing their tonal values, the strong blue background now comes forward, pushing the pale house back.

Landscape Colours

Look at this landscape. Notice that cool colour is used for distant objects. Things far away from you are more indistinct with a blueish tinge. Things close to you are more detailed and strong in colour. Warm colours in the foreground of this landscape bring the objects forward, so that they look as if they are very close to you.

Tree Life

Some artists paint nothing but trees. They are fascinated by their shapes, the movement of the branches in the wind, and the changing appearance of trees through the seasons. On this page, there are some familiar tree shapes, and hints about seasonal colours.

Tree Spotting

You will quickly realize that trees often fit into standard geometric shapes, yet each one can be recognized by its unique combination of colour and outline. Here are some examples.

Coconut Palm
A coconut palm has wonderful fan-like leaves at the top of a tall trunk. Palm fronds are hard-edged and a strong green.

Cypress Cylinder
Think of the tall shape of the cypress in a cylinder and it will help you draw it.

Tall Elm
Elms are tall and have strong branches and thick trunks, with a heavy covering of leaves.

Triangular Pine
Many pines, such as the Christmas tree, are a standard triangle shape.

Blotting and Sponging Leaves

You can give the impression of leaves without painting every one. Here, simply by blotting and sponging. Roughly paint the outline of the foliage with two greens. Quickly, before it dries, blot off excess paint with kitchen tissue. With a sponge, dab in the shadow.

Blowing Blots

This technique is fun and will produce unexpected shapes and colour mixtures. When you have made a blown-blot pattern for a tree's leaves and branches, you can paint in a trunk with a brush.

Seasonal Palette

Tree colours and shapes change through the seasons. Look at these examples.

Winter
Even though the branches are bare, the tree still has a shape. Give an idea of the network of branches, without drawing in every one.

Spring
In spring, first the leaves colour the branches with a yellow tinge, then, as they grow, the foliage thickens and flowers bloom.

Summer
Now the foliage is thick and lush. To give an impression of sunny weather use warm colours.

Autumn
For autumn colours, your palette needs brown, ochre, and red paints to mix and capture the season's rich warm tints.

Red + Yellow + Black

Brown + Yellow + Blue   Pink in two tones

Brown + Red   Brown + Yellow

Brown + Yellow   Blue + Yellow + Purple

1 Load your brush with a watery mix of watercolour. Drop a blob on the page and, with a straw, blow the paint from the blob.

2 The blob will spread and spatter. You can add other colours and blow, making a rich pattern of colours and textures.

3 Add details with a brush dipped in a dryish paint, or use a fibre-tip pen if you prefer.

Skyscapes

When you paint a landscape, the sky often takes up at least half of the picture. Once you start studying the sky, you will find that it is never the same. Even a blue sky is a 'cold' blue in winter and a 'warm' blue on a hot summer's day. Clouds, too, are always changing. There are techniques to help you capture them.

Changing Light

Look how the sky changes throughout the day. The light changes, too.

▲ Morning Sky
Pale, early morning sunlight casts long, soft shadows.

▲ Winter Mixture
A cold blue for a winter's day. Mix blue with white, or water if you are using watercolour.

▲ Summer Sky
Add a touch of crimson red to the blue to warm it for a summer sky. More red and you will have a sunset sky. But don't overdo it.

▲ Midday Sky
With the sun high in the sky, shadows are short and dark. The light is hard and bright.

▼ Evening Sky
As the sun sinks, the world is bathed in soft, golden light. Colours fade and shadows lengthen.

▲ Colourful Clouds
Coloured greys will make your clouds lively. For cloud shadows, mix blue, brown and white.

▲ Stormy Weather
Storm clouds and snow clouds can have a yellowish tinge to their shadows.

◀ Cloud Shadows
Use a blue-grey for the shadows of summer clouds in a blue sky. Mix blue with black.

Cloud Techniques

Blotting Clouds
For fluffy white clouds, apply a watery wash of blue to your sky. Take a tissue and blot up the colour to form white clouds.

Rolling Clouds
Use acrylic paint to apply a flat blue sky. When dry, load your brush with thick white paint and roll the brush over the blue. Add highlights.

Running Clouds
Apply a watery, watercolour blue to an area of sky. While paint is wet, add grey, then black. The colours run into each other to make storm clouds.

Driving Rain
Apply layers of wet washes so that they run into each other, then blot them with tissue. Make the sheets of rain with a tissue wrapped around the brush end.

Sunburst
Build up this dramatic sunburst with careful, layered washes, working from light to dark. Wait for each layer to dry before painting the next.

Making Waves

Foaming Seas
For waves, build up watery poster paint, pale green to dark blue. Then layer over thick white paint and use the end of a brush to 'sgraffito' (scratch) the movement of the foam.

Rippling Waves
With a thin brush, make a series of irregular, curvy lines in black poster paint. When dry, fill the spaces between curves with tones of bright and pale blue, and grey.

Clear Water
Clear, clean water, such as you may find in a swimming pool, is painted here with washes of two blues and greens – patterns of deep and bright tones. Spaces of white paper create highlights.

Water

Water is like a mirror. It reflects on its surface everything around it – grass, trees, sky, and clouds. Like clouds, water is always moving and changing. Look at the difference between a flat pond, a running river, and wave-tossed seas. You can be really experimental and creative when you paint and draw water. Have fun with colours, techniques, and shapes.

Black Reflections
Here, the reflections of boats are coloured in black against washes of blues and grey.

Sunny Reflections
Coloured pencil has been used in this scene. Violet, greens, and browns make up sunny, coloured reflections.

74

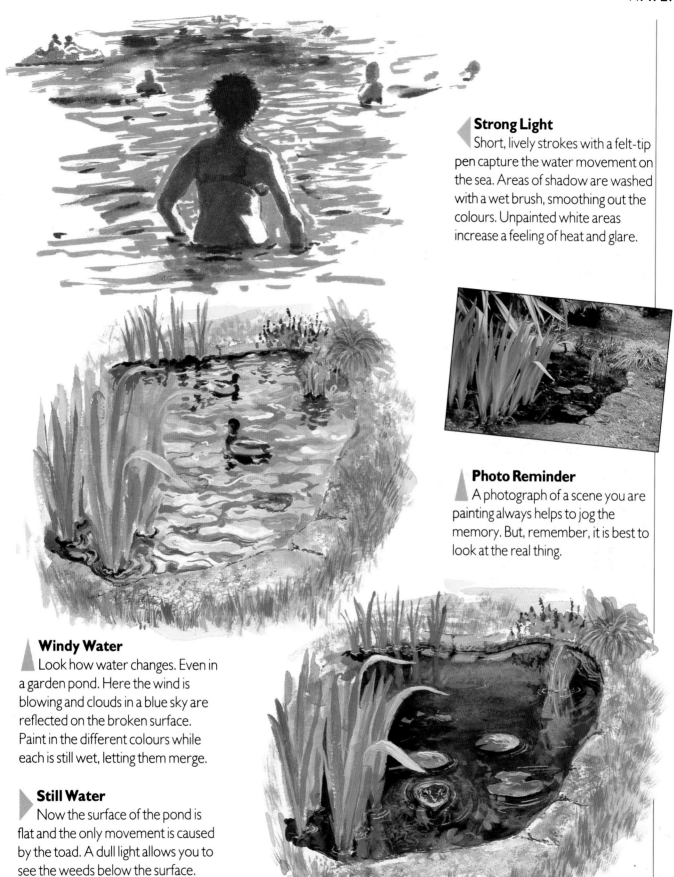

Strong Light
Short, lively strokes with a felt-tip pen capture the water movement on the sea. Areas of shadow are washed with a wet brush, smoothing out the colours. Unpainted white areas increase a feeling of heat and glare.

Photo Reminder
A photograph of a scene you are painting always helps to jog the memory. But, remember, it is best to look at the real thing.

Windy Water
Look how water changes. Even in a garden pond. Here the wind is blowing and clouds in a blue sky are reflected on the broken surface. Paint in the different colours while each is still wet, letting them merge.

Still Water
Now the surface of the pond is flat and the only movement is caused by the toad. A dull light allows you to see the weeds below the surface. Add white to highlight the ripples.

Project: Tree Study

A garden or park offers a whole range of inspiring subjects to paint and draw. Try and find something simple, like this stately line of trees. You will notice how the artist has used some of the landscape 'tricks' you have learnt. Perspective lines through the trees meet at a point on the horizon.

Coloured pencils are excellent for creating textures with hatched lines, built up in layers. The artist works from light to dark, starting with yellow highlights and building up to heavy, hatched, pencil shadows. Note how the changed direction of the hatched strokes adds movement.

1 With a lead pencil, make a light sketch of the composition. It may help if you start by ruling in pale lines of perspective for the trees.

2 Loose strokes of light blue fill the sky. Softly hatch pale yellow and light green on the sunny side of the trees.

3 With the side of the pencil, cross-hatch layers of brown and dark yellow in the background. You can always darken the tones later.

4 Now add more colour to the trees. With short, hatching strokes, go from light green to dark blue. To give movement, vary the stroke direction.

5 Use a ruler to find the straight lines of tree shadows. Then using your dark blue, hatch even strokes against the ruler edge.

6 Loose, free strokes in dark and light green and dark blue create the grassy foreground. Don't cover the paper, as in the sky, but leave some white spaces.

Tree Line
Stand back from your finished picture. You may find you need to deepen a shadow or add a touch of yellow highlight, but be careful not to 'overwork' your drawing.

Beyond the Brush

Sometimes a brush just isn't enough! And neither is a pencil. Here, we introduce you to some new ways of working and give you suggestions for original combinations of techniques you already know. Try out everything to see what ideas you can come up with. There are all sorts of things you can do with paint, and other media, to create a wide variety of unusual effects.

Try adding scraps of material to your landscape. A portrait to paint? How about using a sponge to do it instead of a brush? Fill your paintings with spattering, ragging, and rubbings to show textures – a stony beach or the bark of a tree. These special effects are fun to do and will make your paintings dynamic and unique. Some of the collaging techniques shown on the following pages can be put to use to make an impressive wildlife poster.

Finally, you are invited to explore beyond the real world you can see around you to the realms of ideas and feelings. Subjects like this, which exist only in your mind, free you to express yourself with just colour and form.

Two stages of development in a you

Collage Craft

Collage is fun. It is the art of sticking various materials onto a backing sheet to make a work of art. You can use virtually anything – foil, dried pasta, sweet papers, sequins, string, paper clips. See what you can find. Use a household glue, not paper paste, and collage onto a sheet of thick paper or card. You can add paint or penwork, but let the glue dry first.

Paper Waves

1 Collage can be used for some quite ambitious projects, like this seascape. Make clouds by tearing and cutting black tissue.

Rosy Picture
Sometimes the materials you have found for your collage will suggest an idea to you. Otherwise go through your sketchbook or ideas file for something to try. How about this rose?

Paper Rose
Draw the shapes you need onto coloured paper and cut or tear them out. Torn paper has a soft edge, so use it for the rose petals and leaves. Lay out these shapes before you glue them.

Waxy Rose
The petals of this rose collage were outlined with pen and paint. Some of the leaves are textured by scratching into a layer of wax crayon.

2 Now for the distant waves, fold a piece of paper over three or four times. Cut holes into the folds. Open up and glue the paper below the clouds.

3 The larger waves in front are made by cutting curved pieces of plain coloured paper, then tearing up sheets of speckled blue paper to make wave crests.

4 You may not find all the elements you want in torn or cut paper. Draw what you need – a lighthouse perhaps – cut it out and glue it on.

▲ Stormy Sea
The finished picture is a pleasing mix of hard and soft edges, unusual textures and colours. The collage technique works well here.

Looking at Texture

Rough, smooth, knobbly, spiky – the the world is full of strange and wonderful textures. Of course, you do not have to use an ordinary paintbrush to capture these extraordinary surfaces. You can paint with your fingers, with rags, tissues, and sponges. And to the daring artist, even that old toothbrush is handy and can be put to use.

Leaf Prints

You can make colourful leaf patterns by printing the shapes of real leaves. Use a new leaf for each colour.

1 Use acrylic or poster paint. Apply a thick layer to the upper side of the leaf. Start with a small leaf, one with an interesting shape.

2 Press the leaf down on the paper firmly. Then peel it off quickly. Place one leaf print over another or overlap the prints.

Ragging
For a leafy path or a tree trunk, try ragging. The idea is to dab a scrunched-up rag dipped in a dry, dark colour over dry washes of pale colour.

Sponging
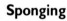
This pebble is built up with layers of sponging. Use a fine sponge and dry paint. Start with dark grey and finish with white.

Blotting

To make subtle changes within a wash of colour, use the blotting technique. After you have laid your colour, soak off patches with a piece of tissue twisted into a point.

Spattering

Dip a toothbrush into paint, then pull your thumb back over the bristles, spattering the paint across the page. Mask with paper any areas you want to keep clean. You can see how this technique has been used for the beach area below.

Rubbing It In

This is a technique that is well-suited to collage but, of course, it can be part of any painted picture.

1 Lay a piece of paper over a textured surface, say stone or wood. Rub over the paper with a pencil or wax crayon.

2 Move the paper slightly and rub again with another colour. Stick this rubbing on drawing paper, then paint and draw over it.

Good Impressions

With this technique, it is hard to tell what is going to happen. You paint onto one surface with thick paint, then press a sheet of paper on top. You can use this method to add texture to an area of flat paint.

1 With thick poster paint, build up an image of a wall. Do this quickly or the paint will dry.

2 Place a sheet of paper over the top and press down over the painted area. The more you press, the more blurred the image will be.

Using Photographs

It is exciting to sketch from life. Fortunately, we all have the opportunity to study birds and many of us can draw from living insects. But we can't always copy from life. Few of us can go on a safari to look at giraffes or tigers. Also, animals, birds, and insects move around so restlessly, it is hard to sketch them. So photographs can really help to increase our knowledge of animals' bodies and movements. Look in magazines and books and collect cuttings for your reference sketchbook.

Bird Shapes
Try to see the shapes of birds as you sketch. Match them to geometric shapes (see pages 20–21). Using photographs to draw from will make it easy to see these shapes and get them right.

In-Flight Pictures
You need to sketch fast as a pigeon or seabird flies by. Get your confidence by studying photos. This will help you when you draw from life.

Paper Bird

This seagull was drawn from a newspaper cutting. Black-and-white photographs often give a clearer idea of an animal's shape, as colour can distract you.

A Photo-Copier

You can make a grid to help you copy, or enlarge, the subject of a photograph with a piece of tracing paper that can be used again and again.

1 On tracing paper, rule up a grid of equal squares to fit over the photo. Use an indelible pen to mark in the lines.

2 Place this grid over the photograph you want to copy. Fix it with masking tape. Then follow the instructions on squaring up (pages 28–29).

Look to Learn

Look for photographs which show different aspects of a bird, animal, or insect. This helps you to understand how its body 'works'.

Lively Locust

Using the three magazine photographs of a locust you can see above, the artist has made a study in coloured pencils. Different photographs were useful for different aspects of the study.

Project: Wildlife Poster

This project uses many of the techniques covered in the previous pages. There is a bit of collage, work from photographs, and some texture techniques. All these combine to make a poster that gives a lot of information through artwork not words. But first you need to gather as much information as possible about a particular animal that interests you. Then you can build up a 'catalogue' of your studies in the form of a poster. You might like to try this for school projects. One advantage to this project is that you can prepare numerous drawings and paintings of the subject, then select the best ones to cut out and use in the finished work. Your poster could show a favourite animal or bird, or a study of wild flowers. The subject chosen here was the life cycle of the frog.

1 Draw the frog's outline and main features on a piece of green paper and cut them out.

2 Make a tracing of the pink parts on its head, legs, and underside. Trace them on to pink paper and cut them out.

3 Assemble all the cut pieces on a blue background sheet and stick them down with paper glue.

4 Draw the details of the frog's markings on to the paper cut-outs with wax crayons and pastels. Make the shapes and colours bold.

5 Do the developing tadpole sketches for the poster on separate sheets of paper, using paint, crayon or pastel.

6 Cut out the smaller drawings and arrange them on a sheet of white cardboard, together with the cut-out frog. When the arrangement looks good, stick down the pieces.

A FROG'S LIFE

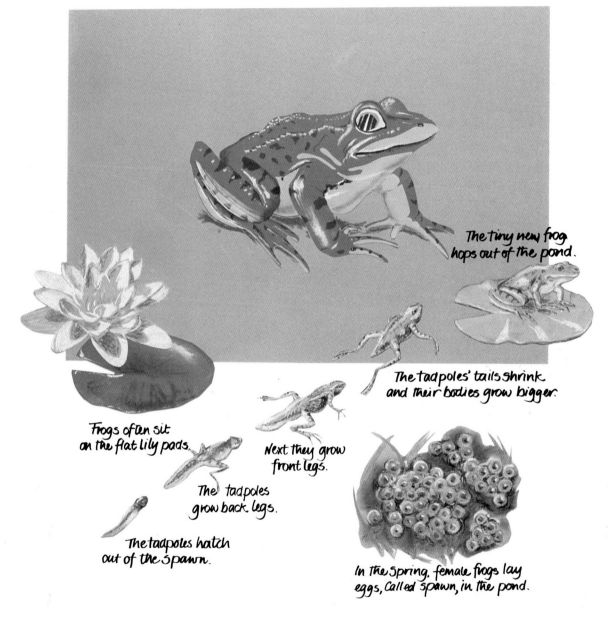

The tiny new frog hops out of the pond.

The tadpoles' tails shrink and their bodies grow bigger.

Frogs often sit on the flat lily pads.

Next they grow front legs.

The tadpoles grow back legs.

The tadpoles hatch out of the spawn.

In the spring, female frogs lay eggs, called spawn, in the pond.

▲ **A Frog's Life**
A poster like this displays the whole of the frog's life-cycle, from spawn and tadpole to adult. To finish it, the artist has added handwritten labels.

Project: Jungle Impression

You may long to express your thoughts just in colour, or paint the mood of a place, not only how it looks. If you do you will be painting an abstract. An abstract painting usually has no people or things you can recognize in it, only colours and shapes which express the artist's ideas and feelings. But you can go halfway to an abstract, as in this project. The artist wanted to paint a tropical jungle. As you see, it is not an exact copy, but uses leaf shapes and colours which suggest tropical vegetation. The picture gives an impression of a jungle. Try the same scene yourself, using your imagination with leaf patterns, collage, fragments of glittery fabric, or magazine photographs of tropical plants and trees.

Local Inspiration
These houseplants inspired the shapes of the forest plants and leaves in this project. There may be something in your home – an ornament or a flower – that gives you the idea for an imaginary place.

1 Sketch in the basic shapes of the large leaves and use wax resist (see pages 32–33) to create the bright green and white pattern.

2 Use oil pastels to fill in the dark background areas. Because these are greasy, they make a surface that resists paint in the same way as candle wax does.

3 Apply washes of acrylic paint very broadly into each of the main colour areas. You can brush one colour over another to make colour changes.

4 Use thicker paint to darken heavy shadows in the background behind the trees. You can brush it over the oil pastel colour used in Step 2.

5 Put in the smaller shapes by painting real leaves and using them as leaf prints (see pages 82–83). You can print them in one colour or multi-colours – use the same technique but apply two or three different colours to one leaf.

6 Add details like these small white flowers by sponging little dabs of thick poster paint over the darker areas already painted. Make sure the paint underneath has dried first, or the colours will run, making the white muddy.

▲ Tropical Trees

The artist has given the impression of a lush jungle with a few shapes and powerful colour. The tree trunks and large leaves of the background come alive with the broken textures of wax and oil pastel resist. Overall, the painting combines a lot of the techniques you have learned – you should be able to achieve something just as good!

Glossary

A

acrylic paint A kind of paint that has a thick, moist texture and comes in a range of bright colours. It can be mixed and thinned with water, but becomes waterproof when dry.

B

bleeding A technique in which colour is washed over the outline of a drawing to increase the feeling of movement.

blending A technique in which one colour is merged into another. In painting, you can brush the colours together while they are still wet. Using coloured pencils, the colours are shaded into one another.

blotting A technique for lightening colours in a painting by lifting wet paint with a tissue or rag.

burnishing A technique in which a final layer of white pencil is shaded over a coloured-pencil drawing to blend and 'polish' the colours.

C

cartridge A type of thin, smoothly finished drawing paper, usually available in white, off-white, and colours.

cast shadow A shadow made when a solid shape blocks the light. The dark shadow of a standing object or figure, for example, is cast on to the wall or floor.

chalk pastel A drawing material made from pigment and gum mixed together and rolled into stick form, then allowed to harden. Chalk pastel is completely dry and becomes loose and crumbly when pressed hard.

collage A technique of making pictures by sticking down paper shapes and other materials which can be cut or torn from different sources. The resulting picture is also called a collage.

composition The arrangement or design of a picture. Elements of composition include lines, shapes, colours, tones, patterns, and textures.

cross-hatching A drawing technique for creating areas of colour and tone by making patterns of closely spaced parallel lines going in opposite directions.

D

dry brush A painting technique that enables an artist to make a fine, 'hairy' texture by spreading out the hairs of a brush between finger and thumb and dragging it through paint.

E

ellipse An oval shape, which is the way a circle looks when you see it on a slant or at an angle.

F

flat colour An area of a painting that is the same colour all over, and does not show any brushmarks or shading.

foreground The area, or plane, in a picture which is nearest to the viewer. A picture can usually be divided into three main planes: the foreground which is closest to you, the middle ground, and the background in the distance.

G

gouache A type of paint made from a gum binder, pigment, and a white 'filler' material like chalk. Gouache paint is smooth, thick, and opaque.

gummed tape Brown paper tape that has a thin coating of gum on one side. When you wet it, it becomes very sticky and remains firmly stuck down when it dries.

H

highlight The brightest point or area on an object, where it reflects light most strongly.

horizon line A dividing line in a painting or drawing that represents the farthest point you can see. For example, in a landscape painting, it is the line between ground and sky. In perspective drawing, it is the line (sometimes imaginary) where the sky meets the *flat* land.

M

modelling In drawing and painting, the method of using light and shadow (by blending or shading, for example) to make the picture look three-dimensional and real.

O

oil pastel A drawing material which consists of pigment mixed with an oil binder, shaped into sticks of colour.

opaque The description of something that cannot be seen through, the opposite of transparent.

P

palette The dish, board or flat slab on which an artist lays out colours to be thinned and mixed for painting. The word is also used to mean the range of colours that an artist uses in a painting.

perspective The drawing method used by artists to show space, distance, and solidity in a picture, converting a view of the three-dimensional world into a two-dimensional image.

pigment The ingredient of a paint which gives it colour.

portrait A painting or drawing that shows a recognizable likeness of a human subject, so that you can tell who the person is by looking at the picture. The term can also be applied to pets and non-living things, such as houses.

pose The position and attitude of a human figure (or animal) as an artist sees it and draws it.

poster paint A type of inexpensive paint, similar to gouache, which is thick and opaque and usually comes in a range of strong colours.

proportions The sizes of different parts of a figure or object in relation to one another.

R

reflection The appearance of colour and light on a surface that comes from a separate surface or object. Sometimes it may be a flash of light, as in a highlight on a shiny surface. Or it could be a whole picture, as seen in a mirror.

rubbings Drawings made by laying paper over a textured surface and rubbing with a crayon.

S

scale The sizes and locations of different things in relation to one another. For example, in a landscape view, a mountain or cliff is a large-scale object, whereas flowers and blades of grass are small-scale features. But in a picture, if the mountain is far away it might appear quite small, while a flower close to you could appear large by comparison.

sgraffito A technique in which lines are scratched, for example with a brush end or pin, into paint to reveal the paper underneath.

shading In drawing, the technique of creating areas of light or dark colours and tones, and blends between them, by rubbing the pencil tip evenly over the paper.

sketch A drawn or painted picture done quickly to give an impression of the subject, rather than a detailed study.

spattering A painting technique in which wet colour is flicked off the bristles of a brush with a finger or thumb to make a pattern of dots and splashes.

sponging A painting technique in which paint is applied with a small piece of sponge rather than a brush to create mottled textures.

squaring up A method of copying a picture in a larger size. It is done by drawing a grid over the original picture, then copying the shapes in each square onto a larger grid.

still life An arrangement of non-living objects which forms the subject of a painting

or drawing, for example, cups and jugs, fruits or vegetables. The term is also used to describe the resulting picture.

study A detailed painting or drawing of a subject. A study is usually a more highly finished picture than a sketch.

T

three-dimensional The quality of the real world, which contains open spaces and solid objects that you can move through and around. A drawing or painting is two-dimensional, that is, flat, so artists have to use methods such as perspective drawing and modelling to re-create three-dimensional effects.

tone A degree of lightness or darkness. In drawing and painting, tone is a measure of relative values – for example, on a scale from white through grey to black, or between a light colour such as yellow and a dark colour such as purple.

W

wash A thin layer of transparent colour, made by mixing paint with a lot of water and brushing it on.

watercolour A type of paint made from pigment mixed with a gum binder. It dissolves easily in water, so is available in moist and hard forms, in tubes or pans.

wax resist A combined drawing and painting technique in which a wax candle or crayon is used to draw, then a wash of paint colour is brushed over the top. The paint cannot settle on the wax, so it flows around the drawing to form a background colour.

Index